A WO
of BALANCE

6 studies for individuals
or groups

Juanita Ryan

Introductions by Linda Shands

With Guidelines for Leaders
and Study Notes

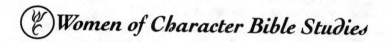
Women of Character Bible Studies

InterVarsity Press
Downers Grove, Illinois
Leicester, England

InterVarsity Press
P. O. Box 1400, Downers Grove, IL 60515, USA
38 De Montfort Street, Leicester LE1 7GP, England

InterVarsity Press® is the book-publishing division of InterVarsity Christian Fellowship®, a student
movement active on campus at hundreds of universities, colleges and schools of nursing in the United
States of America, and a member movement of the International Fellowship of Evangelical Students.
For information about local and regional activities, write Public Relations Dept., InterVarsity Christian
Fellowship, 6400 Schroeder Rd., P.O. Box 7895, Madison, WI 53707-7895.

Inter-Varsity Press, UK, is the book-publishing division of the Universities and Colleges Christian
Fellowship (formerly the Inter-Varsity Fellowship), a student movment linking Christian Unions in
universities and colleges throughout the United Kingdom and the Republic of Ireland, and a member
movement of the International Fellowship of Evangelical Students. For information about local and
national activities write to UCCF, 38 De Montfort Street, Leicester LE1 7GP.

USA ISBN 0-8308-2041-8
UK ISBN 0-85111-382-6

Printed in the United States of America ♾

| 19 | 18 | 17 | 16 | 15 | 14 | 13 | 12 | 11 | 10 | 9 | 8 | 7 | 6 | 5 | 4 | 3 | 2 | 1 |
| 13 | 12 | 11 | 10 | 09 | 08 | 07 | 06 | 05 | 04 | 03 | 02 | 01 | 00 | 99 | 98 | 97 |

Contents

Cast of Characters

Setting the Stage

Each study's introduction takes the perspective of a different character in a continuing story to introduce the theme of each study. Below are the voices behind each introduction.

1 **Stephanie Willis**—a recently widowed mother

2 **Rebecca**—Stephanie's elder daughter

3 **Elly**—Stephanie's grandmother

4 **Laura Fraiser**—Stephanie's supervisor at work

5 **Margaret**—Stephanie's mother

6 **Helga Krueger**—Stephanie's neighbor

Other characters

Stacy—Stephanie's younger daughter

Kara—Laura's daughter

Jerry—Laura's ex-husband

Otto—Helga's husband

Introducing *A Woman of Balance*

The word "balance," especially when used in relationship to the word "woman," brings to my mind an image of a waitress, carrying three or four large trays of food. I imagine the waitress dropping one of the many trays and then questioning her competence. It is an image of trying and failing at the impossible.

Women in our society, and in most societies, are called upon to balance many heavy responsibilities. They are called upon to care for the young, to care for the elderly, to care for the sick, to manage the home, to help provide for the family, and to keep themselves mentally and physically healthy so they can do all these things. With so many concerns to carry at once, how is it possible for women to even think of, much less include in the balance of things, their own needs to be loved and served?

In the story that is a part of this study, we meet Stephanie, her daughters, her employer, her grandmother, her mother and her neighbor. The lives of all of these women are marked by deep loss. And yet, as their lives touch, we find ourselves asking the question differently. We find ourselves asking: "With so many concerns to carry at once, how is it possible for any of us to survive unless we learn to lean on each other? How is it possible to manage at all unless receiving love and service from each other is as much a part of our daily experience as is giving?"

Balance understood in this way no longer brings to mind an image of a juggling act. We are no longer isolated entities who have to somehow manage to carry many heavy trays on our own. The balance we are talking about here has more in common with a sense of flow. Love and care and forgiveness flow to us and through us. Balance in this sense of the word is a picture of a lake, fed by rivers, and in turn, feeding other rivers. It is a picture of women who open their hearts and lives to each other and to God and who are sustained by the flow of love and care between themselves and others and God.

These studies offer the wisdom of Scripture about this kind of balance. The studies are designed to help you develop practical strategies to live in a way that allows for such a flow; a way of being which can make it possible for you to receive even as you are giving, to take in love even as you are reaching out in love, to allow others to serve you even as you are serving. May you come to know the joy of experiencing love and forgiveness and service flowing to you and through you.

Suggestions for Individual Study

1. As you begin each study pray that God will speak to you through his Word.

2. Read the introduction to the study, "Setting the Stage," and respond to the questions that follow it. The story is designed to draw you into the topic at hand and help you begin to see how the Scripture relates to daily life. If there will be a week or more between your studies, then you may want to read all of the introductions in one sitting to get the flow of the ongoing story. This will help if you find that you are having trouble keeping track of all the characters.

3. This is an inductive Bible study, designed to help you discover for yourself what Scripture is saying. Each study deals with a particular passage — so that you can really delve into the author's meaning in that context. Read and reread the passage to be studied. The questions are written using the language of the New International Version, so you may wish to use that version of the Bible. The New Revised Standard Version is also recommended.

4. "God's Word for Us" includes three types of questions. *Observation* questions ask about the basic facts: who, what, when, where and how. *Interpretation* questions delve into the meaning of the passage. *Application* questions (also found in the "Now or Later" section) help you discover the implications of the text for growing in Christ. These three keys unlock the treasures of Scripture.

Write your answers to the study questions in the spaces provided or in a personal journal. Writing can bring clarity and deeper understanding of yourself and of God's Word.

5. Use the study notes at the back of the guide to gain additional insight and information after you have worked through the questions for yourself.

6. Move to the "Now or Later" section. These are ideas for you to freely use in closing your study and responding to God. You may want to choose one of these to do right away and continue working through the other ideas on subsequent days to reinforce what you are learning.

Suggestions for Members of a Group Study

1. Come to the study prepared. Follow the suggestions for individual study mentioned above. You will find that careful preparation will greatly enrich your time spent in group discussion.

2. Be willing to participate in the discussion. The leader of your group will not be lecturing. Instead, she will be encouraging the members of the group to discuss what they have learned. The leader will be asking the questions that are found in this guide.

3. Stick to the topic being discussed. Your answers should be based on the verses which are the focus of the discussion and not on outside authorities such as commentaries or speakers. These studies focus on a particular passage of Scripture. Only rarely should you refer to other portions of the Bible. This allows for everyone to participate on equal ground and for in-depth study.

4. Be sensitive to the other members of the group. Listen attentively when they describe what they have learned. You may be surprised by their insights! Each question assumes a variety of answers. Many questions do not have "right" answers, particularly questions that aim at meaning or application. Instead the questions push us to explore the passage more thoroughly.

When possible, link what you say to the comments of others. Also, be affirming whenever you can. This will encourage some of the more hesitant members of the group to participate.

5. Be careful not to dominate the discussion. We are sometimes so eager to express our thoughts that we leave too little opportunity for others to respond. By all means participate! But allow others to also.

6. Expect God to teach you through the passage being

discussed and through the other members of the group. Pray that you will have an enjoyable and profitable time together, but also that as a result of the study, you will find ways that you can take action individually and/or as a group.

7. It will be helpful for groups to follow a few basic guidelines. These guidelines, which you may wish to adapt to your situation, should be read at the beginning of the first session.

☐ Anything said in the group is considered confidential and will not be discussed outside the group unless specific permission is given to do so.

☐ We will provide time for each person present to talk if he or she feels comfortable doing so.

☐ We will talk about ourselves and our own situations, avoiding conversation about other people.

☐ We will listen attentively to each other.

☐ We will be very cautious about giving advice.

☐ We will pray for each other.

8. If you are the group leader, you will find additional suggestions at the back of the guide.

1

Being and Doing

Psalm 37:1-9

 SETTING THE STAGE:

Stephanie's Story

I kiss his downy head, close my eyes and inhale the sweet clean newborn smell. My favorite moments of the day — before either of us are fully awake. Before the alarm goes off and the fear sets in. Before I remember I'm in this alone.

"Mother! Tell her to give me my sweater."

"It's mine!"

"No, it's not! You borrowed it and never gave it back."

"Mother! Make her stop!"

I groan and look at the clock. *Overslept. I'll be late again.* The clamor stops at my bedroom door. "Mom?"

I hear the fear in my oldest daughter's voice. What if I die too? What would they do then?

The baby whimpers then relaxes into infant dreams. I pull on my terry robe and open the door. "Shh. You'll wake your brother.

"Rebecca, that sweater's filthy. Put it in the laundry hamper. You can borrow my blue one."

"What about me?"

I sigh and ruffle my eight-year-old's untidy curls. "Your red vest is in the closet. It'll match your socks." I hurry toward the kitchen hoping that will end the matter, but rebel-child is right on my heels.

"I don't want to wear that crummy old vest. Why does Becca always get everything?"

I can feel the beginnings of a headache and reach for the coffee pot. *Cold.*

"Because I'm oldest, that's why. Mom, the baby's crying. Can I pick him up?"

"No, me! It's my turn. I never get to do anything. I hate you! I want my dad!"

Her sobs fade behind a slammed bedroom door. Rebecca walks gingerly into the kitchen. The baby is draped over her shoulder, smiling and drooling down the back of my blue sweater.

"She doesn't mean it, Mom. Not the hate you part, anyway."

My ten-year-old knight, the peacemaker. I hug her, ignore the coffee pot and mix a bottle of formula instead.

"Have you eaten?"

She nods. A horn honks in the driveway. She grabs two sack lunches and heads down the hall. "Come on, Stacy, open up. Car pool's here."

I intercept them at the front door, reach around my nursing son and kiss Stacy's tear streaked cheeks. "I love you." I try a smile. She shrugs and follows her sister to the car. A street urchin with her uncombed hair and wrinkled skirt. Too late, I notice her red vest has one pocket ripped off.

The baby wails. I burp and change him, then lay him in the portable bassinet. He accepts the pacifier I swore none of my children would ever have, and I rush into the shower.

I catch the phone on the sixth ring. "We're okay," I reassure my mother. "The girls had a fight though. Stace is still acting out."

"I know it's normal. Look, Mom, I'm late for work again. If I don't get a move on, Laura's going to let me go."

"Yes, I know. But I need that job. Love you too. Bye."

Add two cereal bowls to the pile of dirty dishes in the sink. Mop up grape juice from the kitchen floor. Fill four bottles with formula. Stuff diapers, socks, three extra sleepers in the diaper bag.

The baby howls. He's wet again. I'd cry too, but I don't have time.

---

1. Stephanie is clearly overwhelmed with life's demands. In what ways do you relate to her?

How might the moments of being with her infant give Stephanie strength for all she has to do?

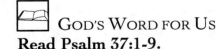 GOD'S WORD FOR US
Read Psalm 37:1-9.

---

2. Compare verses 1-2 and verses 8-9. What are they asking us to let go of?

Why is it important to let go of these things?

3. Verse 3 tells us to "trust in the LORD" and to "do good." Trusting (resting, relying on God) has to do with "being" and doing good, of course, has to do with "doing." How would you describe what it means to trust or to "be"?

How would you describe what it means to "do good"?

4. How would you describe the relationship between trusting and doing good?

Which of these is more difficult for you? Explain.

5. Verses 4-7 continue to ask us to "be." What verbs are used in these verses?

6. Verses 4-6 promise that certain results will come as we allow ourselves to *be* in relationship to God. What promises are made?

7. What experiences (positive or negative) do you have with the instructions in verses 4-7?

8. What might you do to restore balance between being and doing in your life?

NOW OR LATER

Ideas to close your group meeting or personal study or for continued daily reflection.

☐ Make a list of the activities of "doing" you participated in last week. Make a list of the activities of "being" you participated in last week.

Doing   **Being**

Evaluate your lists. How do the lists compare? What, if anything, might you change (add or subtract) this coming week?

☐ Review the verbs that you listed in response to question 5. Spend time each day this week being with God in these ways. Keep a record of your experiences.

☐ Read and reflect on Matthew 6:25-34.

2

....

Loving and Being Loved

John 15:1-17

 SETTING THE STAGE:

Rebecca's Story

I promised Daddy I'd be good and help Mom. I'm trying, but I don't know what to do about Stacy.

"If Daddy were here, he'd be driving us to school, not some old car pool."

She's right, and he'd probably buy us muffins too when he stopped for his latte, but I tell her, "Our other choices are the city bus or our own two feet, and I don't want to walk."

I dig through my lunch sack, pull out a Wipe'n'dry from the last time we had chicken and rip open the packet with my teeth. "Here, wipe your face. Mrs. Andrews will see you've been crying and send you to the counselor's office. If they have to call Mom again, she might lose her job."

"Why's she need that stupid ol' job anyway?"

"To buy your stupid ol' Frosty Pops and your stupid ol' notebook and your stupid ol' shoes."

That got her to smile. "Here, promise you'll be good

today and you can use some of the lipgloss Gran gave me for Christmas."

"The Desert Rose? Mom said you had to save that for special."

"Okay, if you don't want . . ."

She snatches it out of my hand and grins into the little mirror on the side of the case. *This is special*, I want to tell her, but I don't.

"You have each other, Becca," Daddy said, "and you have God. Stick together and you'll be alright."

But he didn't tell me how to make it work. Stacy doesn't want to listen — to Mom, or me, or God. She complains all the time that we never get to go anywhere and her friends can't come over 'cause Mom's never home and besides the house looks like a garbage dump.

"It's partly your garbage," I tell her. "If you'd help clean it up instead of mope around all the time . . ." Everything I say just makes her cry.

What does she know anyway? My friends won't even talk to me. Mom says it's because they don't know what to say and I should "Give them time." It's been six months. How much time do they need? It's not like Kara Fraiser's dad who left her mother and sends Kara expensive presents and takes her places like Disneyland and Wild World Park. The kids can't wait to hear what fun things she did on, "Her weekend away." Kara says her dad will come home soon.

My dad's not coming home. Ever.

Mrs. Bright gave us math homework again, and I pray to God that this time when I open the book I'll understand it. Mom doesn't do algebra either, so I really need a miracle.

Stacy meets me at the fountain like she's suppose to. She left her red vest in the coatroom, but if I make her go back for it, we'll miss our ride. If I don't, she won't have anything warm to wear tomorrow morning. "You can wear my pink sweater," I promise her, "I'll wash it tonight."

I put the sweater in cool water in the sink. We're out of that handwashing stuff, so I use shampoo—Herbal Essence. I lay it on a towel and pray it will be dry by morning.

"Mom's home!" Stacy runs outside to meet her while I hurry to get a bottle ready. The baby's always fussy by the time they get home, and Mom needs to put her feet up for a minute.

"Becca, Becca, look!" Stacy is yanking something out of a Sears shopping bag. "New sweaters. The pink one's mine."

That's okay. I'd rather have the blue. The buttons look like real pearls. Mama kisses the top of my head. I hug her hard to say thanks, then run into the bathroom and lock the door. I don't want her or Stace to see me cry.

---

1. How is Rebecca expressing love for Stacy?

What specific expressions of love might Rebecca need?

How do you see yourself in Rebecca?

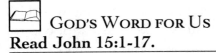 GOD'S WORD FOR US
Read John 15:1-17.

2. Jesus uses the metaphor of a vine and it's branches. As

you picture the image he is using, what do you see about the nature of our relationship with him?

3. In practical terms what does it mean to "remain" or to "abide" (NRSV) in Christ?

4. What does this text say are the results of "remaining" or "abiding" in Christ?

5. What does Jesus say about his relationship with his disciples in verses 9-16?

6. What does this passage teach us about being loved by God?

7. What does it teach us about loving others?

---

8. What is more difficult for you — showing love or receiving love? Explain.

---

9. What barriers are you aware of that stand in the way of your knowing that you are loved by God?

What barriers are you aware of that stand in the way of your showing love to others?

 NOW OR LATER

☐ We can experience the richness of Scripture as we meditate on the images it provides. The following is a simple meditation on the image from this text: Picture yourself as a branch, attached to Christ, a part of him. Picture God, the Father, as the gardener, feeding the soil, watering the roots, with his love. Picture God's love for you flowing into you through Christ, like nutrients flow from a vine into its branches. See yourself as deeply loved and valued by God.

What thoughts and feelings do you have in response to this mediation?

☐ Consider: How might knowing you are loved by God help you to love others?

☐ Read and reflect on 1 Corinthians 13:4-7. As you read, be aware that God is saying this is how he loves you. Then re-read it, realizing this is what it means for us to love each other.

3

Giving and Receiving

Luke 10:38-42

 SETTING THE STAGE:

Elly's Story

I'm not one to question God, but I often wonder why he chose to take Stephie's husband and leave me confined to this darn chair. Old and useless, that's what I am. It don't take much common sense to figure out I was the rightful one to go.

Three babies. Eight and ten and a newborn besides. Poor Margaret's got a heart-load of worry now addin' them to me.

"Who are you talking to, Mama?"

"Myself. You see anyone else in this room?"

"All right, Mama, don't be a grouch. Let's wheel you into the living room. The kids will be here any minute, and I have to see to the stew."

Sometimes I think my Margaret revels in other people's troubles. Not that she likes to see them hurt, but it gives her someone else to do for and nothing makes her happier than that. I used to be the same when I was able.

"Hi, Gran. Hi, Granny Elly." Stacy's kisses are slobbery as ever.

"That's great-grandmother to you, young lady, and don't you forget it."

She grins and rushes out of reach. "I got a new sweater, Gran. Wanna see?"

Stephie's lips just brush my brow. She offers her blanket-wrapped son. "Want to hold him a while? Becca will stay."

Gut shot, as Papa would say. Time was I had one on each hip, another clinging to my skirt and stirred up a meal for ten besides. I wish I could argue, "I won't drop him," but my arms give out and I very well might.

"Set down, Rebecca. Pull up the footstool and talk to me."

She looks toward the kitchen where the others have adjourned. I suppose it now takes three to stir a pot of stew. "They don't need you."

Her brow relaxes. "How are you feeling, Granny Elly?"

"Old." I hike the baby further up my arm. He smiles in his sleep and my heart flutters in response.

"He's really not much trouble." Her wistful smile tells me something else is.

"Then what is?"

"Stacy." It's out before she thinks it, and she covers her mouth with her hand.

"Let me guess. She cries a lot, and throws fits, and won't do her share around the house."

Astonishment. Pure and simple. "How'd you know?"

"I may be cripple, child, but I'm not dumb. She misses her daddy too, you know." I soften my voice. "You have responsibilities: help your mother, keep your grades up, watch out for Stacy. Am I right?"

She nods, leaning forward.

"You cry at night, off by yourself where no one can see." Tears form now, but I keep talking. "Your Mama goes to work, cooks the meals, tends the baby and the house.

She's not got time to cry except in her dreams.

"But Stacy now, that's a different story. She's got no outlet for her grief. No good hard work to soak it up. No pocket she can tuck it in till later. She's got to put it somewhere and home is the safest spot."

I hand her the babe. She settles him on her shoulder like she's been mothering for years. "What should I do, Granny Elly?"

I allow myself a smile. "Well, just what you are doing, I expect. Give her something important to do—she's big enough to tend that boy—then love her and let her cry. She'll come around, God willing. Just give her time."

---

1. What is Elly giving?

What is she receiving?

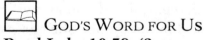 GOD'S WORD FOR US
Read Luke 10:38-42.

2. What are the expectations of each of the characters in this story?

What are they each doing?

---

3. Put yourself in this story. What do you imagine Martha was thinking and feeling?

What do you imagine Mary was thinking and feeling?

---

4. In what ways do you identify with Mary in this story?

---

5. In what ways do you identify with Martha?

---

6. How does Jesus respond to each woman?

What is the significance of Jesus' responses?

7. What thoughts and feelings do you have regarding Jesus' responses?

8. If you took an inventory in your own life, what would you say about the balance between giving and receiving? Explain.

9. What might you do to restore a better balance between giving and receiving in your life?

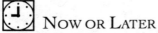 NOW OR LATER

☐ What barriers exist that make it difficult for you to receive from others?

What barriers exist that make it difficult for you to give to others?

☐ Make a specific plan to give and to allow yourself to receive this week.

What reactions do you have to making such a plan?

☐ Read Philippians 2:22-30. Reflect on Paul's ability to give and receive.

4

Forgiving and Being Forgiven

Colossians 3:12-15

 SETTING THE STAGE:

Laura's Story

Recently widowed. Two young children. Seven months pregnant. Overqualified for the job. All good reasons why I shouldn't have hired Stephanie Willis.

I look at my watch and turn to wait on a customer. She leaves with two novels and a book on child care. Six customers later, still no Stephanie. I remember my other reservations: Needs full-time work and the bookkeeping takes twenty hours a week, max. Then I thought, what if she takes over the register too? That will leave me more time for ordering, taking inventory and helping customers on the floor.

I remember praying, then deciding, "Okay, Lord, Stephanie it is."

Stephanie only missed one day of work before she had the baby. Then three weeks maternity leave.

"I hate to leave him in daycare," she said on the phone. "All those germs. You wouldn't know a private sitter, would you?"

I remember the trauma of leaving Kara, even with my mother. "Bring him," I told her. "He should do fine until he starts to crawl. You can worry about child-care then."

"Oh, Laura, you're the best. He sleeps three hours at a stretch and hardly ever cries." Sounds of sniffling, blowing her nose.

I picture myself in the months after Jerry left. It hasn't been easy building up this business. Jerry left when Kara was six. I've done it on my own. With mucho help from God: a Christian banker, supportive friends, a mother who is always willing to babysit. The list is endless.

Stephanie finally shows. The girls had a spat and the baby has colic. We both skip lunch. At five o'clock I lock up and we both hurry home to fix dinner for our kids.

❊   ❊   ❊

Kara picks a piece of bacon fat out of her green beans and feeds it to the dog. "Rebecca Willis don't like me much."

"Doesn't," I correct her automatically. "Why?"

She shrugs. "I think it's because I still have a dad and she don . . . doesn't. She's jealous!" Kara's eyes light up.

I make a mental note to talk to Jerry about the way he's spoiling her. Now that he's found someone else he wants to marry, he's buttering up his daughter, waiting for the right time to spring it on her. Bribery. It has to stop.

I choose my words carefully. "Maybe if you didn't brag so much about the things Dad buys you, and the places you go, you might find Rebecca will make a good friend."

"Well, I don't say it to her, Mom. She just overhears me telling my friends."

❊   ❊   ❊

"Tired is a state of being," I tell Stephanie a few days later. "You won't see straight until he's three."

"Actually Stacy's the hardest. She misses her dad so much and takes it out on me."

I nod in sympathy. At least I have only one to raise. They'd have to cart me to the loony bin with three.

The baby is good when they are here, but he really slows her down. *So she's been late a few times.* I tell myself it doesn't matter. It won't hurt me to run the register once in a while.

"The board of health is going to condemn my house," she laments.

"I have to go to the store, we're down to peanut butter and mayonnaise."

She never asks for extra money, so I give her time. But it's not enough. More often than not Stephanie drags in with white-ringed eyes and shaking hands. She can't wait on customers like that, but she's keeping up the books okay.

Then one day she doesn't show. Doesn't even call till after ten.

"Chicken pox. Both of them!" She can't get their fevers down.

I ring up a box of greeting cards and grab the phone again. The school nurse sounds exhausted. "Epidemic . . . Pick-up Kara . . . Ten days."

Now I'm really in a jam. With my mother visiting friends in Florida, there's nothing else to do but close the store.

---

1. In what ways does Laura's experience with loss turn into compassion for Stephanie?

How have you seen this dynamic at work in your own life?

 GOD'S WORD FOR US
Read Colossians 3:12-15.

2. This text refers to the readers as "God's chosen people, holy and dearly loved" (v. 12). Take a minute to put your name in this verse and to see yourself as chosen by God, holy and dearly loved. What thoughts and feelings do you have as you mediate on this picture of who you are?

3. The text goes on to ask us to "clothe ourselves" with a way of being in this world. List the qualities that are called for in verse 12.

4. How might these qualities flow out of knowing you are forgiven?

How might they flow out of forgiving others?

5. Verse 13 reminds us to "forgive as the Lord forgave" us. What is the relationship between knowing we are forgiven and forgiving others?

6. Which comes more easily to you, knowing you are forgiven or extending forgiveness to others? Explain.

7. What barriers might stand in your way of knowing you are forgiven?

What barriers might stand in your way of extending forgiveness to others?

8. The text continues by reminding us to "put on love" (v. 14). What is the relationship between knowing we are forgiven, forgiving others and putting on love?

---

9. Verse 15 tells us: "Let the peace of God rule in your hearts, since as members of one body you were called to peace." What is the relationship between forgiveness and being at peace as members of one body?

How have you experienced this?

 Now or Later

☐ Ask God to remove the barriers to receiving his forgiveness. Spend some time in prayer, picturing those barriers being removed, knowing you are forgiven. Write a response to God, expressing gratitude for his forgiveness.

☐ Ask God to remove the barriers which hold you back from extending forgiveness to someone in your life. Picture yourself releasing your fear and anger and hurt to God. Picture God acknowledging your pain. And picture God loving and forgiving the person who hurt you. Then write a letter to the person(s) who came to mind, expressing whatever is in your heart and mind at this time. (You don't have to send the letter.)

☐ Read and reflect on Ephesians 4:32.

5

....

Serving and
Being Served

John 13:1-17

 SETTING THE STAGE:

Margaret's Story

"Why, Stacy, you look pretty as a picture in that sweater. Come here and give us a kiss. . . . Stephanie, sit down and put your feet up, I just need to add a drop or two of thickening to the stew."

"Mmmm, Gran, is that cornbread I smell?"

"What else? You know your Granny Elly, she has to have bread with every meal." I lower my voice so it doesn't drift into the other room. "She's been so contrary lately. Maybe holding the baby will sweeten her some. 'Course I'd be grouchy too if I had to endure that much pain, poor soul.

"Stacy, hand me that ladle, there's a lamb."

"Which dishes do you want, Mama? I'll set the table."

"You'll do no such thing, Stephanie. You do enough at home. The least I can do is give you a day off once in a while.

"Stacy dear, I believe I saw a cantaloupe melon on the vine this morning. Doesn't that sound good?"

"I'll get it, Gran."

I wait until she's out the door before voicing my concern. "Is she getting enough sleep, Stephanie? I called the girls after school yesterday and she sounded terrible. I almost went right over, but your granny needed me to rub her feet. It has to be hard on them to go home to an empty house. Don't you think . . ."

"Mom, we've been through this. It's just too far for the girls to come here after school. I get home an hour after they do."

There—I've hurt her feelings again. You'd think I'd learn. "I know, dear. I just wish . . . Ah, well." I hug her shoulders and drop a kiss on her silky brown hair. I remember holding her when she was just Stacy's age and kissing away the hurts. If only it could be that simple now.

I count out service for five and set the kitchen table. "How's Rebecca? How's she doing in school?"

Becca walks in the kitchen and answers me herself. "I'm fine, Gran. And school's fine too, except for algebra."

"Algebra! Isn't that a high school class?"

Becca has the most beautiful smile. She's going to be a heartbreaker some day. And no father to guard her.

I take the baby and check his feet and hands. *Nice and warm.* "Stephanie, he's so precious. How will you ever be able to leave him?"

"I don't know, Mom. I'm praying for someone to come to the house."

I should keep quiet, but I can't. "You have to be so careful, I saw an article in the paper just the other day . . ."

She looks wounded again.

"I know, Mom. I thought I'd ask around at church. Laura says I can keep him at the store as long as he'll stay in one place. That's another six months at least."

Six months? "You know dear, maybe I could sell this

house and get a place closer to you and the girls. Then Mama and I could have the baby during the day and the girls could come after school. We'd have a meal ready at night, so all you would have to do is get them to bed."

I never did understand how Stephanie could laugh and cry at the same time. Mama used to do the same thing. She rarely does either now.

Stephanie wraps me in a hug and nuzzles the baby's neck. "Put him in his carrier, Mom. I'll wheel Granny in."

Is that a yes, or a no, or a maybe? Well, it's not my way to push, but something has to be done before she wears herself out.

---

1. What resistance to being served do you see in Stephanie?

What reasons might there be for this resistance?

 GOD'S WORD FOR US
Read John 13:1-17.

2. What does the text tell us about Jesus' reasons for washing his friends' feet at this time?

3. What thoughts and feelings do you have as you read of Peter's reaction to Jesus (vv. 6-9)?

4. If you put yourself in the story as one of the disciples, how might you react to Jesus coming to you with a basin of water and a towel, kneeling before you and lovingly washing your feet?

5. What do you see as the value of doing simple acts of service for others?

6. What value is there in allowing oneself to receive acts of service from others?

7. Read Jesus' comments in verses 14-17 again. What is Jesus teaching us about servanthood?

8. What barriers might exist for you in serving others?

What barriers exist for you in allowing others to serve you?

 NOW OR LATER

☐ Write a prayer, asking God to remove the barriers you have identified to serving and being served.

☐ Consider the possibility that you may be serving others in a compulsive ("I have to," "I ought to") way. And consider the possibility that you may not be receptive to receiving help or service from others. This creates an unhealthy situation in which resentment and pride can take root. What misbeliefs about yourself or others or God might keep you stuck in this kind of a lifestyle?

☐ Spend some time putting yourself more fully in this story. Picture Jesus wanting to show you the depth of his love for you by offering you a gentle act of kindness. He comes to you with a towel and a basin of water, and kneels at your feet. He removes your shoes, washes your feet and dries them, all the time communicating how much he values you and loves you. Write your response to this meditation.

☐ If you are studying in a group, divide into twos or threes and wash each other's feet. Talk together about the experience.

☐ Read and reflect on Matthew 11:28-30.

6

Weeping and Rejoicing

Psalm 126

 SETTING THE STAGE:

Helga's Story

To knead and braid the dough, it is therapy for me. On Mondays I make Strudel and it's no trouble to bake extra. A small thing and it makes the young ones smile.

We never had children, Otto and I. Not that they weren't wanted.

"Goodness knows I don't want to interfere," I told him just the other night, "but to hear that baby crying and those little girls with such sad faces. Our young neighbor must be exhausted."

"Ya, but what can you do? It is life, Helga."

Otto is right. I pray for them and take a meal now and then.

On Monday she doesn't go to work at all. I take the pastry over early.

"Oh, Mrs. Krueger, thank you. I'm sorry I can't ask you in. The girls have chicken pox and the house is such a mess."

"If there's anything I can do . . ." I go back next door, but it doesn't feel right.

On Tuesday she is hanging sheets on the line. "What will you do about work?" I ask across the fence.

"Laura, Mrs. Fraiser, had to close the shop. Her daughter's sick too. There's no one else to watch them."

"I will come. Otto and I are immune." I do not even hesitate, it is only right. "I am a nurse — two years retired, but I still know what to do. Have Mrs. Fraiser bring the other child here."

Her eyes brighten. "Oh, we couldn't ask you. Three of them? That's too much."

"You did not ask. I volunteered. I will just go tell my Otto."

On Wednesday I take potato pancakes and a pot of chicken soup. The girls are propped up in their room like spotted puppies in a pen. Their fevers are down and they are tired of laying still.

"TV for just one hour. Then I will read to you."

They look at each other and giggle. They think they are too big.

One hour and the kitchen is finally clean. The living room is next, but first the promised story.

"Hans Brinker?" They do not know him, but after two pages they sit enchanted by the tale.

Lunch now. Then back to bed. Clean sheets, fresh air from the open window. They sleep the afternoon away.

"More soup on the stove, and homemade rolls."

"Mrs. Krueger, the house is so clean! And dinner too. We can't thank you enough."

"Helga, please." Her smile is all the thanks I need.

Tomorrow a casserole with baby carrots and homegrown peas. Her bedroom needs turning out. I'll ask permission first.

I show Stacy how to mend her skirt and sew a button on her sweater. Kara and Rebecca learn to follow recipes and catch up on their schoolwork.

Kara hates English and algebra is hard for Rebecca. I suggest they help each other. Ten short days and they are back in school. I miss their chatter, their attentive little faces, and have promised to find another book to read to them.

Five months later we have read three other classics. They come over after school for cocoa and a treat. Stephanie often lingers for a chat, but the baby is restless, wants down on all fours. I didn't realize they could move that fast.

"He's tired of the playpen." Stephanie stirs sugar into her tea. "I can't keep him at work much longer."

"Ya, that is a problem." I scoop him off the floor and plop a bite of strudel into his open mouth. "There now. Helga is here. You just leave him to me."

---

1. What impact might Helga's gifts of love and service have on Stephanie, Stacy, Rebecca and Laura?

What benefit might giving these gifts have for Helga?

Stephanie and Helga have suffered different losses in life. How have their times of weeping brought them together in a way that can bring rejoicing?

GOD'S WORD FOR US
Read Psalm 126.

2. What caused the people in this story to weep?

What caused them to rejoice?

3. How do they describe their experience of weeping?

How do they describe their experience of rejoicing?

4. What do verses 5-6 suggest is the relationship between weeping and rejoicing?

5. How have you seen this to be true in your own life?

6. What do you do to express sorrow?

_____

7. What do you do to express joy?

_____

8. Which is more difficult for you? Explain.

_____

9. How might you add to your ways of expressing your sorrow and your joy?

 NOW OR LATER

☐ The psalm suggests expressing our sorrow and joy with each other. Spend some time sharing joys and sorrows in your group or with a close friend.

☐ Express your current experience of sorrow or of joy in the form of a prayer, poem, collage, drawing, song or some other form of creative expression.

☐ Read and reflect on Romans 12:15.

Guidelines for Leaders

My grace is sufficient for you. (2 Corinthians 12:9)

If leading a Bible study is something new for you, don't worry. These studies are designed to be led easily. As a matter of fact, the flow of questions through the passage from observation to interpretation to application is so natural that you may feel that the studies lead themselves.

You don't need to be an expert on the Bible or a trained teacher to lead a Bible discussion. The idea behind these inductive studies is that the leader guides group members to discover for themselves what the Bible has to say. This method of learning will allow group members to remember much more of what is said than a lecture would.

This study guide is flexible. You can use it with a variety of groups—student, professional, neighborhood or church groups. Each study takes about forty-five minutes in a group setting with the possibility of extending the time to sixty minutes or more by adding questions from "Now or Later."

There are some important facts to know about group dynamics and encouraging discussion. The suggestions listed below should enable you to effectively and enjoyably fulfill your role as leader.

Preparing for the Study

1. Ask God to help you understand and apply the passage in your own life. Unless this happens, you will not be prepared to lead others. Pray too for the various members of the group. Ask God to open your hearts to the message of his Word and motivate you to action.

2. Read the introduction to the entire guide to get an overview of the subject at hand and the issues which will be explored. Also read through the introductions to each study to get the flow of the continuing story that runs through the guide and to get familiar with the characters. Be ready to refer the group to the list of characters on the back of the contents page if they have questions about the story.

3. As you begin each study, read and reread the assigned Bible passage to familiarize yourself with it.

4. This study guide is based on the New International Version of the Bible. It will help you and the group if you use this translation as the basis for your study and discussion.

5. Carefully work through each question in the study. Spend time in meditation and reflection as you consider how to respond.

6. Write your thoughts and responses in the space provided in the study guide. This will help you to express your understanding of the passage clearly.

7. It might help you to have a Bible dictionary handy. Use it to look up any unfamiliar words, names or places. (For additional help on how to study a passage, see chapter five of *Leading Bible Discussions*, InterVarsity Press.)

8. Take the "Now or Later" portion of each study seriously. Consider how you need to apply the Scripture to your life. Remember that the group will follow your lead in responding to the studies. They will not go any deeper than you do.

Leading the Study

1. Begin the study on time. Open with prayer, asking God to help the group to understand and apply the passage.

2. Be sure that everyone in your group has a study guide. Encourage the group to prepare beforehand for each discussion by reading the introduction to the guide and by working through the questions in the study.

3. At the beginning of your first time together, explain that these studies are meant to be discussions, not lectures. Encourage the members of the group to participate. However, do not put pressure on those who may be hesitant to speak during the first few sessions.

4. Have a group member read the story in "Setting the Stage" at the beginning of the discussion or allow group members some time to read this silently. These stories are designed to draw the readers into the topic of the study and show how the topic is related to our daily lives. It is merely a starting point so don't allow the group members to get bogged down with details of the story or with trying to make a literal connection to the passage to be studied. Just enjoy them.

5. Every study begins with one or more "approach" questions, which are meant to be asked before the passage is read. These questions are designed to connect the opening story with the theme of the study and to encourage group members to begin to open up. Encourage as many members as possible to participate and be ready to get the discussion going with your own response.

Approach questions can reveal where our thoughts or

feelings need to be transformed by Scripture. That is why it is especially important not to read the passage before the approach question is asked. The passage will tend to color the honest reactions people would otherwise give because they are, of course, supposed to think the way the Bible does.

6. Have a group member read aloud the passage to be studied.

7. As you ask the questions under "God's Word for Us," keep in mind that they are designed to be used just as they are written. You may simply read them aloud. Or you may prefer to express them in your own words.

There may be times when it is appropriate to deviate from the study guide. For example, a question may have already been answered. If so, move on to the next question. Or someone may raise an important question not covered in the guide. Take time to discuss it, but try to keep the group from going off on tangents.

8. Avoid answering your own questions. If necessary, repeat or rephrase them until they are clearly understood. An eager group quickly becomes passive and silent if they think the leader will do most of the talking.

9. Don't be afraid of silence. People may need time to think about the question before formulating their answers.

10. Don't be content with just one answer. Ask, "What do the rest of you think?" or "anything else?" until several people have given answers to the question.

11. Acknowledge all contributions. Try to be affirming whenever possible. Never reject an answer. If it is clearly off-base, ask, "Which verse led you to that conclusion?" or again, "What do the rest of you think?"

12. Don't expect every answer to be addressed to you, even though this will probably happen at first. As group members become more at ease, they will begin to truly interact with each other. This is one sign of healthy discussion.

13. Don't be afraid of controversy. It can be very stimulating. If you don't resolve an issue completely, don't be frustrated. Move on and keep it in mind for later. A subsequent study may solve the problem.

14. Periodically summarize what the group has said about the passage. This helps to draw together the various ideas mentioned and gives continuity to the study. But don't preach.

15. "Now or Later" can be used in a variety of ways depending on the time available to you and the interests of your group members. You may want to discuss an application question or idea and make some commitments. Or you may want to allow five minutes or so of quiet reflection within the group time so that people can journal their responses. Then, ask simply, "What did you experience (and/or learn) as you journaled?"

You will want to use at least one of these ideas to wrap up the group time, but you may want to encourage group members to continue working through other ideas throughout the week. You can continue discussing what has been learned at your next meeting.

16. Conclude your time together with conversational prayer. Ask for God in following through on the commitments you've made.

17. End on time.

Many more suggestions and helps are found in *Small Group Leaders' Handbook* and *The Big Book on Small Groups* (both from InterVarsity Press). Reading through one of these books would be worth your time.

Study Notes

Study 1. Being and Doing. Psalm 37:1-9.

Purpose: To explore ways of balancing being and doing.

Question 2. The first two verses of this text tell us to let go of "fretting" and "envy." A closer look shows us that we are being asked to let go of our anger and our anxiety about the seeming success of people who do evil. When people behave in destructive ways toward others and there seems to be no justice, we are often tempted to lose hope in a sense of meaning in life, and we may begin to doubt whether God cares, or whether God is even paying attention. It is important to let go of anxiety, anger and envy because they rob us of our peace and reflect our fear that God has abandoned us. God has not abandoned us. God is paying attention. We can leave the fate of those who do evil in God's hands. We can be at peace.

Verses 8-9 instruct us to let go of anger and fretting because it only leads to evil and because justice is in God's hands. We can live a life judging, condemning, seeking revenge and growing bitter, or we can let go of anger and of fretting and know peace of mind.

Question 3. Consider the way you envision "being" or "trusting" and the way you envision "doing."

"Trusting" or "being" might be seen as: (1) remember-

ing that God is God and that we are not God, (2) believing
we can depend on God to care for us and for others, and
(3) resting in this truth and being at peace.

"Doing" might be seen as actively remembering that
we have a part in God's work and that we are called upon
to live in relationship to God and others in ways which
are loving, respectful, compassionate and kind.

Question 4. The relationship between being and doing, or
trusting and doing, might be seen as knowing we do not have
to be God; we are only asked to be God's children. There
are things we have to leave in God's hands, things we have
to depend on God for. And there are things we are called
upon to do. But even the things we are called upon to do we
need to do in dependence on God, remembering that we are
creatures and that God is the Creator.

Consider the flow or the balance in your life between
being and doing. Is it more difficult to rest in God's care
or to do what you believe you have been called to do?

Question 5. The verbs which are used in relationship to
"being" or "trusting" are: delight (in the Lord), commit
(to the Lord), trust (in the Lord), be still (before the
Lord) wait patiently (for the Lord), let go of worry (do
not fret).

Question 6. The promises that are made in relation to
"being" are: "he will give you the desires of your heart";
"he will do this"; "he will make your righteousness shine
like the dawn and the justice of your cause like the
noonday sun."

Question 7. Consider: What struggles have you had with
committing, being still, waiting and so on? What joys
have you experienced in "being" these ways?

Question 8. Brainstorm ways you might practice the art
of being and ways you might practice the art of "doing

good." Consider as well the value of having both in one's life and ways to keep these in balance.

Study 2. Loving and Being Loved. John 15:1-17.

Purpose: To work toward a balance between giving and receiving love.

Question 2. Use your imagination as you think about the relationship between a vine and a branch. The vine of a grapevine reaches into the soil to draw up water and nourishment that it sends into the branches so they can grow strong and healthy. The vine provides the stabilizing force for the branches. The vine holds the branches together. The branch depends on the vine for all these things. As the branch receives water and nourishment from the vine, it grows and it produces grapes. It explodes with life and joy. It expresses the essence of its nature.

Jesus is teaching us that we need him. We need to hold onto him, to stay close to him, to drink deeply of his gifts of life and love. It is the relationship of a young child to a caring parent. It is a relationship of love and attachment and dependency.

Question 3. If you are leading a group, ask members to describe their own experience with abiding in Christ. How do they do this? For some it may be a certain time each week or each day in prayer and study. For others it may be a frequent, ongoing experience of acknowledging God, or asking for help or wisdom and direction. Others might have other experiences of what this means in their life. Emphasize that the heart of abiding is growing in awareness of God's unfailing love for us.

Question 4. The text tells us that the results of abiding in Christ include: (1) bearing "fruit" (showing love to others), (2) God abiding in us, (3) being able to ask for what we need and having it given to us, and (4) experiencing joy.

Question 5. In verses 9-16 Jesus makes several statements about his relationship with his disciples. He calls his disciples "friends." He tells them that he loves them like his Father loves him, that he wants them to know joy, that he tells them everything that his Father tells him.

Question 6. Reflect on what this text tells us about what it means to be loved by God. Love gives what is needed (as a branch gives water, nourishment and stability). Love wants joy for the one it loves. Love self discloses (Jesus says "I love you," and he tells them what his Father tells him). Love is respectful (I call you friends). The text teaches us that in the same way God the Father loved Jesus, Jesus loves us. It teaches us to remain in (stay close to, stay aware of) God's love by following the commandment to love each other. And it teaches us that this will bring us joy.

Question 7. Reflect on what this text tells us about what it means to love each other. Jesus tells us to love each other in the way he has loved us: by meeting each other's needs, by wanting joy for each other, by saying "I love you" and sharing our hearts and minds with each other, by being respectful and valuing of each other (as friends). The text teaches us that what God asks of us is to love each other. By doing this, we stay close to God's love, we participate in God's love, we grow in our awareness, understanding and experience of God's love.

Question 9. Barriers to knowing we are loved by God are numerous. These barriers might include believing we do not deserve love and believing God is harsh. Barriers to showing love to others might include fear, judgment and distrust.

Study 3. Giving and Receiving. Luke 10:38-42.

Purpose: To learn how to bring a balance between giving to others and receiving from others.

Question 3. Martha was entertaining a very important guest. She was preparing a meal for him and for the friends and family who would be getting together for the occasion. She was working hard and no one was helping her. Mary was sitting and talking with Jesus, while Martha was doing all the work.

Martha was probably feeling stressed, pressured, frustrated and even angry. When she asked Jesus to tell her sister to lend her a hand she probably felt quite justified in doing so. But Jesus responded by telling Martha that she was worried about many things, and then by telling her that Mary had made the better choice! Martha may have be bewildered, shocked and confused. If she didn't do all this work, who would? If both she and Mary sat around and talked instead of working, how would anything ever get done?

Mary may have felt shamed by Martha's request of Jesus. After all, Martha did not come to her directly and ask her for help, but instead went to Jesus and asked him to use his influence to get Mary to do something. If Jesus had sent Mary off to the kitchen she probably would have felt shamed by him as well, and may have come to believe that time spent in conversation, in relationship, in receiving was not as valuable as time spent in doing and giving.

Question 5. If you are leading a group, encourage members to discuss their longing for relationship and their longing to receive from the company of others. Allow them to discuss any other ways they may identify with Mary.

Question 6. Most will probably readily identify with

Martha—with the pressure, stress and frustration she felt. **Question 7.** Jesus acknowledged Martha's stress and anxiety. And he acknowledged Mary's choice to spend time interacting with him. In doing this Jesus was acknowledging the deepest longings of all of our hearts— our longing to be loved. He was giving that longing and our pursuit of it top priority. He was saying it is critical to receive love. Martha, too, could have been sitting with Jesus. She, too, could have been receiving from him. He had not asked for a gourmet meal. Bread and cheese and fruit would have done fine.

Sometimes we hide our needs and longings behind doing and giving. It is vulnerable to admit that we need help or love or care or comfort from Jesus or from others. But we do. And it is critical to our spiritual and emotional well-being that we acknowledge this truth.

Study 4. Forgiving and Being Forgiven. Colossians 3:12-15.

Purpose: To explore the relationship between giving and receiving forgiveness.

Question 2. Focus on each of the descriptive words Paul uses: chosen, holy, dearly loved.

If you are leading a group, encourage members to spend a moment in silence, picturing themselves as dearly loved by God, forgiven, chosen by him. Allow participants to describe their reactions to these realities.

Question 3. Paul asks us to clothe ourselves with compassion, kindness, humility, gentleness and patience.

Question 4. These qualities flow out of knowing we are forgiven, because the awareness of God's forgiveness in our lives dissipates judgment and fear and allows us to open our hearts to others. When we see God's forgiveness for ourselves, we see it for all. These qualities flow out of our forgiveness of others because forgiveness requires that we let go of anger and resentment and see others as valuable and lovable.

Question 5. Encourage members to discuss freely the relationship they have experienced between being forgiven and forgiving. Henri Nouwen writes that compassion grows in us when "we realize that nothing human is alien to us, that the roots of all conflict, war, injustice, cruelty, hatred, jealousy, and envy are deeply anchored in our own heart" (*The Way of the Heart* [New York: Ballentine, 1981], p. 20). When we realize this and thus forgive rather than judging others, our hearts are made tender with love, and the qualities listed in verse 12 are a natural outcome.

Question 6. Participants may have difficulty with one more than the other, or you may find both difficult in certain circumstances.

Question 7. The barriers to knowing we are forgiven might include: fears that God is harsh or punitive, believing what we did was somehow "too bad" to forgive, fears that they have not repented "right" or "enough." Sometimes bringing these fears and beliefs out into the light can help to dispel them.

Barriers to forgiving others might include: not being ready to let go of anger, feeling what the other person did was "too bad" to forgive, not wanting to minimize the pain that was inflicted by the other, not wanting to "pretend" things are forgiven when they are not. Forgiveness is often a process of facing the hurt inflicted, acknowledging the pain and the feelings that accompany the hurt, and giving the hurt and the feelings to God—letting it go into God's hands. A recommended resource for working through the process of forgiveness is *Recovery from Bitter-ness* by Dale and Juanita Ryan (Downers Grove, Ill.: InterVarsity Press, 1992).

Question 8. Love and forgiveness are nearly synonymous. When we know we are loved, we know we are forgiven. When we see another person through the eyes of love, we are prepared to forgive them. Give examples of this.

Question 9. Peace is the result of forgiveness. When there is hurt or conflict, and the hurt or conflict is resolved with forgiveness, bitterness does not grow between people. The result is peaceful relationships. Give examples of this.

Study 5. Serving and Being Served. John 13:1-17.
Purpose: To bring a balance between serving others and allowing others to serve them.

Question 2. Reasons can be found throughout the passage. The text tells us that Jesus washed his friends' feet at this time because he loved them, and he wanted to show them how much he loved them. Jesus did this knowing he was about to be crucified, knowing he was about to say goodbye to them.

The true basis of service is love for the other person. It is not to establish control or superiority, but to express value, respect and love for the person being served.

Question 3. Responses to Peter's spontaneous refusal to let Jesus wash his feet and his reversal to asking Jesus to wash all of him will vary from person to person. Peter's open expressiveness can be very touching, because much of what he says and does in the stories of the Gospels speaks for all of us.

Question 4. Imagine yourself as Jesus' friend at the time or imagine Jesus doing this right now. Jesus did this to express his deep love and valuing of his friends. Jesus loves and values us to this same extent. If you are leading a group, remind them of these things and allow people to respond to these thoughts with gratitude, disbelief, amazement, or whatever reactions they may have.

Question 5. The value in doing simple acts of service are many. They include having an opportunity to remember the intrinsic value of the other person, having an opportunity to express that valuing and to express our love and God's love, and growing in our awareness of God's love for us and for all others.

Question 6. The value of receiving acts of service are also many. They include: experiencing that we are loved and valued (and that we are lovable and valuable), growing in humility, and acknowledging our need for and our gratitude for others.

Question 7. Jesus is teaching the value of servanthood which is expressed in specific acts and based in genuine love and humility.

Question 8. In serving, there may be barriers of time, energy, overload, feeling inadequate, not knowing what to say or do. In being served, there may be barriers of shame, pride and not wanting to be a burden.

Study 6. Weeping and Rejoicing. Psalm 126.

Purpose: To discuss the value of both weeping and rejoicing.

Question 2. The people in this story wept because they were taken away from family, friends and home as captives. They rejoiced when God brought them back to their homes and set them free.

Question 3. The experience of weeping is described as

"sowing in tears." The experience of rejoicing is described as "being like men in a dream," having "mouths filled with laughter and tongues with songs of joy," being "filled with joy," and "returning with songs of joy."

Question 4. The text suggests that weeping may precede rejoicing. Healing is often a painful process, which includes sowing tears of grief. But the end result of this process is joy. Difficult times come and we grieve and even despair, but healing and restoration and new life follow losses and sorrows, so that we rediscover the joy of life.

Question 5. If you are leading a group, allow time to share stories of times when sorrow gave way to joy.

Questions 6-7. Explore the ways you express sorrow and joy, and the ways you avoid expressing these feelings.

Question 8. It is most likely that people will identify the expression of sorrow as more difficult than the expression of joy. As a society, and as a Christian culture, we tend to value joy more than sorrow. But actually, both may be difficult to experience and express. We can suppress our joy as well as our sorrow. They both need physical expression.

Question 9. Brainstorm ways you might more fully express your joy and your sorrow. This might include writing prayers or journal entries, singing (or other use of music), art work, talking, dancing and writing letters.

InterVarsity Press Bible Studies by Juanita Ryan

Women of Character Bible Studies
A Woman of Balance
A Woman of Beauty
A Woman of Blessing
A Woman of Confidence

LifeGuide® Bible Studies
Psalms II

Life Recovery Guides by Juanita and Dale Ryan
Recovery: A Lifelong Journey
Recovery from Abuse
Recovery from Addictions
Recovery from Bitterness
Recovery from Broken Relationships
Recovery from Codependency
Recovery from Depression
Recovery from Distorted Images of God
Recovery from Distorted Images of Self
Recovery from Family Dysfunctions
Recovery from Fear
Recovery from Guilt
Recovery from Loss
Recovery from Shame
Recovery from Spiritual Abuse
Recovery from Workaholism

Novels by Linda Shands

Seasons Remembered Series
A Time to Keep
A Time to Embrace
A Time to Search
A Time to Speak

All books and Bible studies are published by InterVarsity Press and are available from your local Christian bookstore. Visit our web site at www.ivpress.com for more information and for "The Small Group Doctor" column. E-mail us with your feedback on this guide at doctor @ivpress.com.